MARVEL

STICKER ART PUZZLES

THUNDER BAY
P·R·E·S·S
San Diego, California

Thunder Bay Press
An imprint of Printers Row Publishing Group
9717 Pacific Heights Blvd., San Diego, CA 92121
www.thunderbaybooks.com • mail@thunderbaybooks.com

© 2022 MARVEL

Printers Row Publishing Group is a division of Readerlink Distribution Services, LLC.
Thunder Bay Press is a registered trademark of Readerlink Distribution Services, LLC.

Correspondence regarding the content of this book should be sent to Thunder Bay Press, Editorial Department, at the above address.

Thunder Bay Press
Publisher: Peter Norton
Associate Publisher: Ana Parker
Art Director: Charles McStravick
Senior Developmental Editor: Diane Cain
Editor: Jessica Matteson
Production Team: Beno Chan, Rusty von Dyl, Mimi Oey

Produced by Judy O Productions, Inc.
Author: Steve Behling

ISBN: 978-1-66720-038-5

Printed, manufactured, and assembled in Dongguan, China

26 25 24 23 22   1 2 3 4 5

CONTENTS

INTRODUCTION

FACE FRONT, TRUE BELIEVERS! YOU NOW HOLD IN YOUR HANDS ONLY THE MOST MOMENTOUS, MIGHTY, AND MAGICAL STICKER BOOK EVER ASSEMBLED--AND THAT'S SAYING SOMETHING! BUT WHEN YOU'RE DEALING WITH THE LIKES OF SPIDER-MAN, THE GUARDIANS OF THE GALAXY, THE AVENGERS, MS. MARVEL, AND MORE, WHAT ELSE DO YOU EXPECT?

FROM THE FIRST APPEARANCE OF THE HUMAN TORCH IN 1939, MARVEL HAS HAD ITS FINGER ON THE PULSE OF POPULAR CULTURE AND COMIC-BOOK FANDOM FOR 80 YEARS--AND COUNTING.

ON THESE PAGES YOU'LL FIND FIFTEEN SPECTACULAR STICKER PUZZLES DEPICTING VINTAGE MARVEL COMIC BOOK COVERS STARRING YOUR FAVORITE MARVEL SUPER HEROES FROM THE 1930S THROUGH THE 1980S. WITH MORE THAN ONE HUNDRED STICKERS PER PUZZLE, YOU'LL BECOME YOUR OWN HERO AS YOU PIECE TOGETHER ICONIC COVERS, ILLUSTRATED BY SOME OF THE MOST IMPORTANT NAMES EVER TO GRACE THE PAGES OF COMIC BOOKS CREATED BY AN ARRAY OF AMAZINGLY TALENTED ARTISTS FROM COMICS HISTORY. ALONG THIS HERO'S JOURNEY, YOU'LL LEARN MORE BONUS FACTS ABOUT THESE COOL CHARACTERS THAN YOU CAN SHAKE A WEB AT!

NOW IT'S TIME TO TURN THE PAGE AND PIECE TOGETHER THE MOST PULSE-POUNDING ASSORTMENT OF MARVEL COMICS COVERS YOU'VE EVER SEEN.

'NUFF SAID!

INSTRUCTIONS

ON EACH PUZZLE PAGE, YOU'LL FIND A GRID. USE THE STICKERS TO REVEAL STUPENDOUS SUPER HEROES ON HISTORIC COMIC BOOK COVERS FROM THE MARVEL UNIVERSE.

HOW TO SOLVE THE PUZZLES

EACH STICKER PUZZLE FEATURES A FRAMED "OUTLINE" OF THE COMIC BOOK COVER YOU WILL PIECE TOGETHER. ENCLOSED IN THE OUTLINE ARE GEOMETRIC SPACES THAT OFFER HINTS WHERE EACH PIECE GOES. APPLY EACH STICKER TO ITS CORRESPONDING SHAPE IN THE OUTLINE. THE STICKERS CAN BE MOVED IN CASE YOU MAKE A MISTAKE. USE YOUR SUPER POWERS TO WORK YOUR WAY THROUGH THE PUZZLES!

THE STICKERS START ON PAGE 52. ALL OF THE PAGES IN THE BOOK ARE PERFORATED, SO YOU CAN TEAR OUT THE PUZZLE, STICKERS, AND SOLUTIONS PAGE TO LAY THEM OUT AS YOU WORK. YOU CAN SOLVE THE PUZZLES SOLO OR ROUND UP YOUR SUPER HERO TEAM AND EACH TACKLE A PUZZLE. IF YOU NEED A LITTLE HELP, NUMBERED SOLUTIONS BEGIN ON PAGE 36, OR USE THE PUZZLE KEY ON THE BACK FLAP FOR REFERENCE.

PUZZLES

THE HUMAN TORCH

MARVEL COMICS #1 INTRODUCED
THE WORLD TO MARVEL'S FIRST SUPER HEROES: THE UNDERSEA *SUB-MARINER* AND THE FIERY *HUMAN TORCH*. BOTH HAD AN EDGE TO THEM. THE CHARACTERS WERE OFTEN PORTRAYED AS ANTI-HEROES, FIGHTING AGAINST A SYSTEM THAT THREATENED THEIR PERSON, AS WELL AS THOSE AROUND THEM.

WHEN WE FIRST ENCOUNTER THE HUMAN TORCH, WE FIND HIM DORMANT, INSIDE THE LABORATORY OF PROFESSOR PHINEAS HORTON. HORTON IS PLEASED TO PRESENT TO THE PRESS *THE WORLD'S FIRST ANDROID!* HOWEVER, WHEN HE REMOVES THE CHAMBER THAT ENCASES THE ANDROID AND IT COMES INTO CONTACT WITH OXYGEN, THE ANDROID'S BODY *CATCHES FIRE!* THE ASSEMBLED PRESS URGES HORTON TO DESTROY THE ANDROID BEFORE SOME "MADMAN" CAN USE IT TO *DESTROY THE WORLD.*

AFRAID THEY MAY BE RIGHT, HORTON AGREES TO ENCASE THE ANDROID IN A STEEL TUBE, CAPPED WITH CONCRETE ON EITHER END. BUT THERE'S A SLOW LEAK, AND SURE ENOUGH, THE ANDROID CATCHES FIRE AND THE HUMAN TORCH ESCAPES. CONFUSED BY THE WORLD AROUND HIM, HE IS USED BY A COUPLE OF CRIMINALS IN AN *INSURANCE/ARSON SCHEME.* THE TORCH FOILS THEIR PLANS AND *A HERO IS BORN.*

THANKS TO EXPOSURE TO *NITROGEN GAS,* THE HUMAN TORCH IS ABLE TO CONTROL HIS FLAME AND CAN APPEAR IN HIS REGULAR ANDROID FORM *"FLAMING ON"* AT WILL. PROFESSOR HORTON BELIEVES HE CAN MAKE MONEY FROM THE HUMAN TORCH AND HIS ABILITIES, BUT THE ANDROID REFUSES TO BE USED BY ANOTHER HUMAN AND DEPARTS.

THE FIRST MAJOR CROSSOVER IN COMICS HISTORY OCCURRED WHEN *THE HUMAN TORCH* CAME FACE TO FACE IN A CITY-WIDE BATTLE AGAINST THE *SUB-MARINER* IN *MARVEL MYSTERY COMICS #9* (JULY 1940).

THE HUMAN TORCH WOULD GO ON TO JOIN *THE INVADERS,* A TEAM OF WORLD WAR II-ERA SUPER HEROES (INCLUDING CAPTAIN AMERICA AND HIS OLD FOE, THE SUB-MARINER), FIGHTING *AGAINST THE AXIS POWERS.*

THE ORIGINAL ANDROID HUMAN TORCH SERVED AS THE INSPIRATION FOR THE JOHNNY STORM HUMAN TORCH IN *THE FANTASTIC FOUR.*

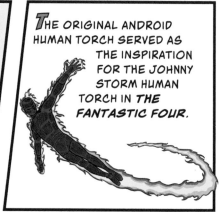

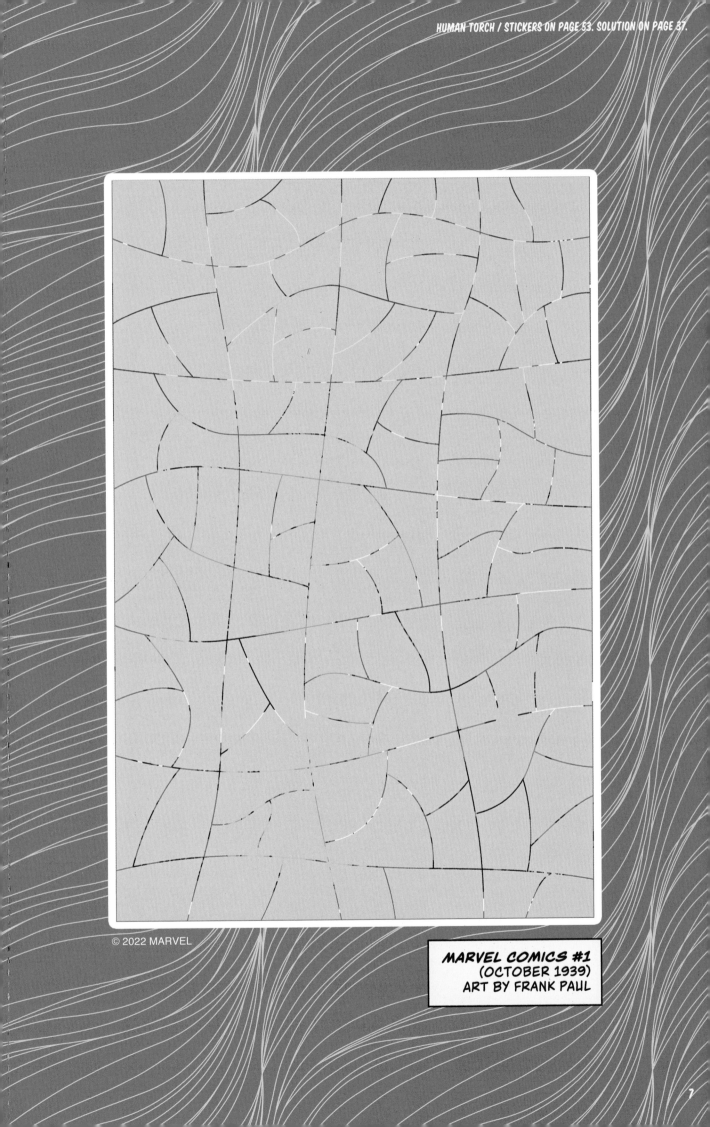

MARVEL COMICS #1
(OCTOBER 1939)
ART BY FRANK PAUL

DOCTOR STRANGE

THE BRILLIANT SURGEON

DOCTOR **STEPHEN STRANGE** FOUND HIS CAREER CUT SHORT FOLLOWING A TRAGIC AUTOMOBILE ACCIDENT. WITH THE NERVES IN HIS HANDS DAMAGED BEYOND REPAIR, STRANGE LEARNED THAT HE WOULD NEVER AGAIN BE ABLE TO PERFORM SURGERY. THE VAIN, EGOTISTICAL STRANGE REFUSED TO ACCEPT THIS AND TRAVELED THE WORLD **SEEKING A CURE.**

HIS QUEST LED HIM TO THE ANCIENT ONE, WHO PURPORTEDLY HAD AN **EERIE POWER** THAT COULD RESTORE HIS DAMAGED NERVES. BUT UPON MEETING THE ANCIENT ONE AND HIS TWISTED DISCIPLE BARON MORDO, STRANGE DISCOVERED SOMETHING **WITHIN HIMSELF:** A DESIRE TO HELP HUMANITY AND TO PROTECT THE WORLD FROM THE MOST DIRE OF THREATS. HE STUDIED THE MYSTIC ARTS AND, IN TIME, BECAME **DOCTOR STRANGE,** MASTER OF THE MYSTIC ARTS.

NOW OPERATING FROM HIS **SANCTUM SANCTORUM** IN NEW YORK CITY'S GREENWICH VILLAGE, STRANGE MUST DO BATTLE WITH UMAR, A SINISTER SORCERESS FROM ANOTHER DIMENSION. IN ORDER TO DEFEAT HER, THE ANCIENT ONE COMMANDS STRANGE TO RELEASE A BIZARRE BEING NAMED ZOM.

THE ANCIENT ONE WAGES **MAGIC WAR** AGAINST UMAR ON THE FIELDS OF STONEHENGE, MERELY BUYING TIME UNTIL DOCTOR STRANGE CAN ARRIVE WITH ZOM. THE CREATURE MANAGES TO THWART UMAR'S PLANS, BUT NOW THE ANCIENT ONE AND DOCTOR STRANGE HAVE TO FIGURE OUT **WHAT TO DO ABOUT ZOM!**

THE NEXT SECOND, AMIDST CASCADING TONGUES OF **CRIMSON FIRE,** A FIGURE OF **REGAL BEARING** SUDDENLY APPEARS...

THE POWERS WHICH YOU LEARNED DURING YOUR YEARS OF EXILE HAVE MADE YOU **OVER-BOLD,** KALUU...TO SEEK TO QUENCH THE UNFALTERING FLAMES OF THE FALTINE!

DR. STRANGE! YOU DARE TO **RETURN?**

THE NEED FOR FLIGHT IS **PAST,** BRAZEN ONE! NOW MUST BE THE TIME OF THE **FINAL RECKONING!** PREPARE FOR **BATTLE!**

IN HIS FIRST APPEARANCE IN **STRANGE TALES #110** (JULY 1963), DOCTOR STRANGE ENCOUNTERS **NIGHTMARE,** A **MYSTICAL FOE** CAPABLE OF HAUNTING THE DREAMS OF HIS VICTIMS.

DOCTOR STRANGE WOULD GO ON TO FORM HIS OWN SUPER TEAM WITH HULK AND THE SUB-MARINER, KNOWN AS **THE DEFENDERS.** THE SILVER SURFER WOULD SOON JOIN THEIR RANKS AS WELL.

DOCTOR STRANGE BECAME EARTH'S SORCERER SUPREME FOLLOWING THE DEATH OF THE ANCIENT ONE AT THE TENTACLES OF THE EXTRA-DIMENSIONAL CREATURE SHUMA-GORATH IN **MARVEL PREMIERE #10** (SEPTEMBER 1973).

(MAY 1967)
ART BY MARIE SEVERIN

STRANGE TALES #156
(MAY 1967)
ART BY MARIE SEVERIN

THE MIGHTY THOR

WHILE VACATIONING IN NORWAY, AMERICAN DOCTOR **DONALD BLAKE** STUMBLED UPON AN UNBELIEVABLE SIGHT: STONE-LIKE ALIENS FROM SATURN HAD ARRIVED ON EARTH. THEY WERE BUT A **SCOUTING PARTY**, PAVING THE WAY FOR A FULL-ON INVASION OF THE PLANET. UNFORTUNATELY FOR BLAKE, THE ALIENS DISCOVERED THE DOCTOR SPYING ON THEM AND GAVE CHASE.

SEEKING REFUGE IN A **MAZE OF CAVES** IN THE NORWEGIAN CLIFFS, BLAKE JOURNEYED DEEPER AND DEEPER, ONLY TO FIND THE EXIT BLOCKED BY AN ENORMOUS, SEEMINGLY UNMOVABLE BOULDER. WITH HIS ALIEN ADVERSARIES SURE TO FIND HIM, BLAKE NEARLY GAVE INTO DESPAIR. THEN HE DISCOVERED AN **ANCIENT, GNARLED CANE** INSIDE A SECRET CHAMBER AND TRIED TO USE IT AS A LEVER TO MOVE THE BOULDER. WHILE THE CANE WAS UNABLE TO MOVE IT, BLAKE STRUCK IT AGAINST THE BOULDER IN ANGER.

A **BOLT OF LIGHTNING** STRUCK, AND SUDDENLY BLAKE FOUND HIMSELF TRANSFORMED INTO THE ASGARDIAN **GOD OF THUNDER, THOR**! THE CANE WAS NOW AN ENCHANTED HAMMER, BEARING THESE WORDS: "WHOSOEVER HOLDS THIS HAMMER, IF HE BE WORTHY, SHALL POSSESS THE POWER OF...THOR."

THOR HAD LITTLE DIFFICULTY BEATING THE INVADING ALIENS AND FORCING THEM TO ABANDON THEIR PLANS OF **CONQUERING THE EARTH**. STRIKING HIS HAMMER ON THE GROUND, THOR RETURNED TO HIS IDENTITY AS DOCTOR DONALD BLAKE AND WONDERED WHAT CHALLENGES HE WOULD SOON FACE.

WHILE THE ONLOOKERS WATCH IN MUTE, UNCOMPREHENDING AWE, THE MIGHTY *THOR* SLAMS HIS ENCHANTED HAMMER DOWN UPON THE PAVEMENT WITH AN IMPACT FELT HALFWAY ACROSS THE STATE!!

WHOOM!

JOURNEY INTO MYSTERY WITH THE MIGHTY **THOR** WHEN MEET THE IMMORTALS!

BLAKE HAD TO MAINTAIN **PHYSICAL CONTACT** WITH THE HAMMER IN ORDER TO RETAIN HIS POWER AS THOR. IF HE LET GO OF THE MALLET FOR MORE THAN 60 SECONDS, HE WOULD REVERT TO HIS **HUMAN FORM**.

THOR FIRST APPEARED IN THE PAGES OF **JOURNEY INTO MYSTERY**. THE CHARACTER PROVED SO POPULAR THAT THE TITLE OF THE BOOK WAS CHANGED TO **THE MIGHTY THOR** WITH ISSUE #126 (MARCH 1966).

IT WOULD BE REVEALED IN **THE MIGHTY THOR #159** THAT THOR HAD BEEN GIVEN THE "DONALD BLAKE" IDENTITY BY HIS FATHER, ODIN, KING OF ASGARD, AS A **PUNISHMENT** IN ORDER TO TEACH HIS BRASH SON THE **LESSON OF HUMILITY**.

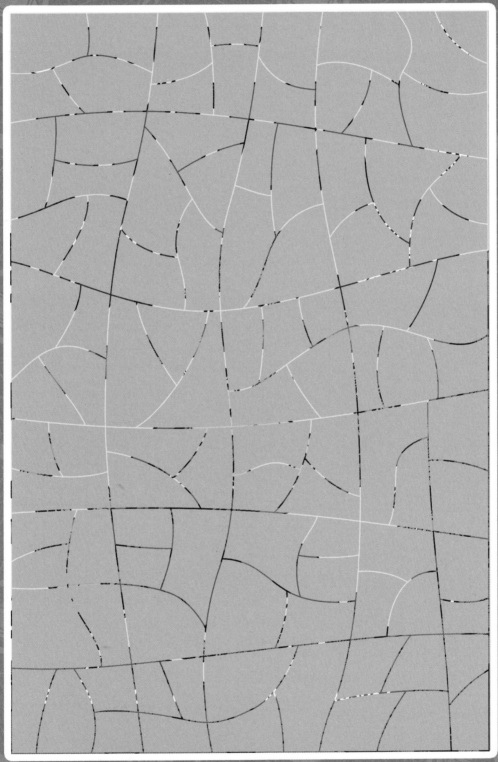

© 2022 MARVEL

JOURNEY INTO MYSTERY #83
(AUGUST 1962)
ART BY JACK KIRBY (PENCILS),
JOE SINNOTT (INKS),
STAN GOLDBERG (COLORS),
ARTIE SIMEK (LETTERS)

THE INVINCIBLE
IRON MAN

GENIUS INVENTOR ANTHONY STARK

SEEMED TO HAVE IT ALL: WEALTH, FAME, AND THE ENVY OF PEOPLE THE WORLD OVER. STARK HAD A *LUCRATIVE CONTRACT* WITH THE UNITED STATES GOVERNMENT TO DEVELOP WEAPONS FOR THEIR ARMED FORCES, AND HE PROVIDED AMAZING TECHNOLOGY *FAR AHEAD OF ITS TIME.*

INVITED BY THE U.S. TO WITNESS A TEST OF HIS TECH IN ACTUAL COMBAT CONDITIONS, STARK ACCIDENTALLY TRIGGERED A *JUNGLE BOOBY TRAP.* KIDNAPPED BY THE ENEMY, THE GRAVELY WOUNDED STARK DISCOVERED THAT HE HAD SHRAPNEL LODGED NEAR HIS HEART--HE WOULD BE DEAD IN A WEEK. THE ENEMY PROMISED TO OPERATE ON STARK IF HE WOULD CREATE A *TERRIBLE WEAPON* FOR THEM.

KNOWING HIS FOES HAD NO INTENTION OF SAVING HIS LIFE, STARK HAD OTHER PLANS. WITH THE HELP OF ANOTHER PRISONER, PROFESSOR HO YINSEN, STARK INSTEAD BUILT A *SUIT OF ARMOR* THAT WOULD PREVENT THE SHRAPNEL FROM REACHING HIS HEART. BUT THE SUIT WOULD HAVE OTHER PURPOSES TOO. AS HO POWERED UP THE SUIT AND GAVE HIS LIFE TO PROTECT STARK, *IRON MAN WAS BORN.*

INSIDE THE IRON MAN ARMOR, STARK SCATTERED THE ENEMY FORCES, AVENGING HO AND FREEING HIMSELF FROM THEIR CLUTCHES. RETURNING TO THE U.S., STARK BECAME KNOWN FAR AND WIDE AS *THE INVINCIBLE IRON MAN.*

> WITH ALL HIS STRENGTH-- ALL HIS POWER--HE LACKED THE *ONE* THING THAT MIGHT HAVE *SAVED* HIM--
>
> THE THING THAT IS NOW SAVING *ME*--
>
> JET-ASSISTED *SPEED*--AND THE ABILITY TO *SOAR*-- TO FLY OUT OF HARM'S WAY BEFORE THE FINAL CATACLYSM--

*T*HE ORIGINAL *IRON MAN ARMOR* WAS A BULKY SUIT, GRAY IN COLOR. BY THE TIME OF HIS SECOND APPEARANCE IN *TALES TO ASTONISH #40* (APRIL 1963), TONY STARK WOULD CHANGE THE COLOR OF THE ARMOR TO GOLD.

*F*OR YEARS, TONY STARK KEPT HIS IDENTITY AS IRON MAN A *SECRET FROM THE PUBLIC.* INSTEAD, THE WORLD BELIEVED THAT IRON MAN WAS HIS BODYGUARD!

*I*RON MAN WOULD BECOME PART OF THE *MARVEL SUPER HEROES ANIMATED SERIES* (1966) ONLY THREE YEARS AFTER HIS DEBUT. HIS ADVENTURES WOULD APPEAR ALONGSIDE THOSE OF *CAPTAIN AMERICA, HULK, THOR,* AND *SUB-MARINER.*

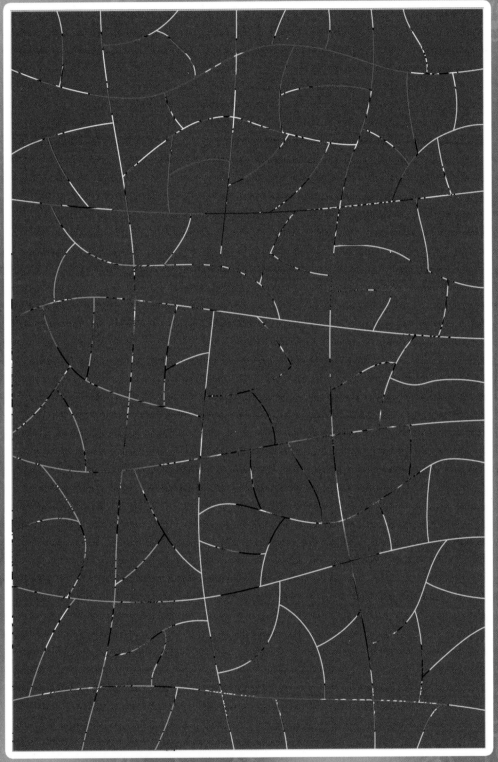

TALES OF SUSPENSE #39
(MARCH 1963)
ART BY JACK KIRBY, DON HECK

ANT-MAN and THE WASP

SCIENTIST HANK PYM (A.K.A. ANT-MAN) IS APPROACHED BY THE WEALTHY PROFESSOR VERNON VAN DYNE AND HIS DAUGHTER, JANET, TO HELP HIM TEST AN **EXPERIMENTAL DEVICE** THAT WOULD ALLOW HIM TO MAKE CONTACT WITH BEINGS FROM **ANOTHER GALAXY.** PYM DECLINES, STATING THAT HIS FIELD OF EXPERTISE IS BIOLOGY.

UNKNOWN TO PYM, VAN DYNE WOULD TEST THE DEVICE HIMSELF, UNWITTINGLY BRINGING AN ALIEN FROM THE PLANET KOSMOS TO EARTH. A CRIMINAL ON HIS OWN WORLD, THE CREATURE **KILLED VAN DYNE** THEN ESCAPED. HIS DAUGHTER, JANET, THEN CONTACTED PYM, AND SOON ANT-MAN WAS INVOLVED IN ONE OF HIS **MOST DANGEROUS ADVENTURES.**

REALIZING THAT HE WOULD NEED A PARTNER TO DEFEAT THE THREAT OF THE **ALIEN FROM KOSMOS,** PYM ENLISTED THE AID OF JANET VAN DYNE. IMPLANTING WINGS IN HER BACK THAT WOULD APPEAR WHEN SHE SHRUNK DOWN TO TINY SIZE, PYM DUBBED HIS NEW PARTNER **THE WASP.**

TOGETHER, PYM AND VAN DYNE TACKLED THE CREATURE FROM KOSMOS, AND WITH THE HELP OF HIS ANTS, ANT-MAN AND THE WASP WERE ABLE TO TURN BACK THE TERRIBLE THREAT TO THEIR WORLD. WITH THE **MISSION ACCOMPLISHED,** PYM WAS APPROACHED BY AN FBI AGENT WHO WANTED TO BE HIS PARTNER. PYM TURNED THE OFFER DOWN, FOR HE HAD ALREADY FOUND THE PERFECT PARTNER IN THE WASP!

HANK PYM WOULD CHANGE HIS IDENTITY FROM ANT-MAN TO **GIANT-MAN** IN **TALES TO ASTONISH #49** (NOVEMBER 1963) AS HE BATTLED A FOE CALLED THE LIVING ERASER.

BOTH ANT-MAN AND THE WASP WOULD GO ON TO BE FOUNDING MEMBERS OF **THE AVENGERS,** ALONGSIDE IRON MAN, THOR, AND HULK. WASP WOULD BECOME THE LEADER OF THE TEAM IN **THE AVENGERS #217.**

JANET VAN DYNE REMINDED HANK PYM OF HIS FIRST WIFE, MARIA, A **FORMER POLITICAL PRISONER** MURDERED BY THE HUNGARIAN GOVERNMENT.

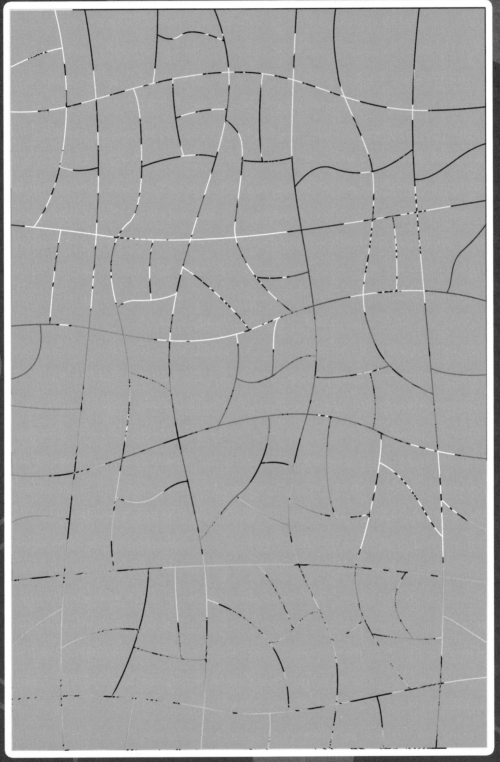

TALES TO ASTONISH #44
(JUNE 1961)
ART BY JACK KIRBY (PENCILS),
DON HECK (INKS), STAN GOLDBERG
(COLORS), ARTIE SIMEK (LETTERS)

the AMAZING SPIDER-MAN

TO SAY THAT PETER PARKER WASN'T THE MOST POPULAR STUDENT AT MIDTOWN HIGH WOULD BE AN UNDERSTATEMENT. PETER DID HIS BEST TO IGNORE THE *CRUEL TAUNTS* OF HIS CLASSMATES WHO CONSIDERED HIM TO BE A *SCIENCE NERD.* HIS BEST FRIENDS WERE HIS AUNT MAY AND UNCLE BEN, WHO ENCOURAGED THEIR NEPHEW'S *SCIENTIFIC PURSUITS.*

PARKER'S LIFE WAS FOREVER TURNED UPSIDE DOWN THE DAY HE DECIDED TO ATTEND A DEMONSTRATION IN *RADIOACTIVITY.* AS HE WATCHED THE EXPERIMENT ALONG WITH THE CROWD, PARKER FAILED TO NOTICE A TINY SPIDER DESCENDING ON A WEB, CROSSING THROUGH THE RADIOACTIVE RAYS. DYING, THE SPIDER FELL ONTO PARKER'S HAND AND *BIT HIM.*

SUDDENLY FEELING DIZZY, A *STRANGE NEW POWER* SURGED THROUGH PARKER. HE FOUND THAT HE NOW HAD *INCREDIBLE STRENGTH,* BEING ABLE TO LEAP GREAT DISTANCES AND CLIMB WALLS. SOMEHOW, MIRACULOUSLY, THE BITE HAD GIVEN PARKER THE PROPORTIONATE ABILITIES OF A SPIDER! HE CREATED A COSTUME AND DUBBED HIMSELF *SPIDER-MAN.*

AT FIRST, PARKER CHOSE TO USE HIS POWERS AS A PERFORMER FOR MONETARY GAIN, TO HELP HIS STRUGGLING AUNT AND UNCLE. AFTER ONE PERFORMANCE, PARKER FAILED TO STOP A BURGLAR. LATER THAT NIGHT, THE HORRIFIED TEEN WOULD LEARN THAT HIS BELOVED UNCLE HAD BEEN KILLED BY THE SAME BURGLAR HE DID NOT DEFEAT. USING HIS NEWFOUND ABILITIES TO CAPTURE THE BURGLAR, PARKER LEARNED THAT WITH *GREAT POWER,* THERE MUST ALSO COME *GREAT RESPONSIBILITY.*

IN HIS SECOND APPEARANCE IN *THE AMAZING SPIDER-MAN #1,* THE WALL-CRAWLER EARNED THE ETERNAL WRATH OF *DAILY BUGLE* PUBLISHER *J. JONAH JAMESON,* WHO VOWED TO USE THE POWER OF HIS NEWSPAPER TO BRING DOWN SPIDER-MAN.

*S*PIDER-MAN WORE THE SAME COSTUME FOR YEARS, UNTIL HE TRAVELED TO THE ALIEN BATTLEWORLD. THERE, HE RECEIVED AN ALL-BLACK COSTUME THAT HE WORE FOR A SHORT TIME BEFORE DISCOVERING IT WASN'T A COSTUME BUT *A LIVING CREATURE!*

*T*HAT *"ALIEN COSTUME"* WOULD ONE DAY ENCOUNTER DISGRACED JOURNALIST EDDIE BROCK, AND TOGETHER THEY WOULD BECOME ONE OF SPIDER-MAN'S MOST NIGHTMARISH FOES--*VENOM!*

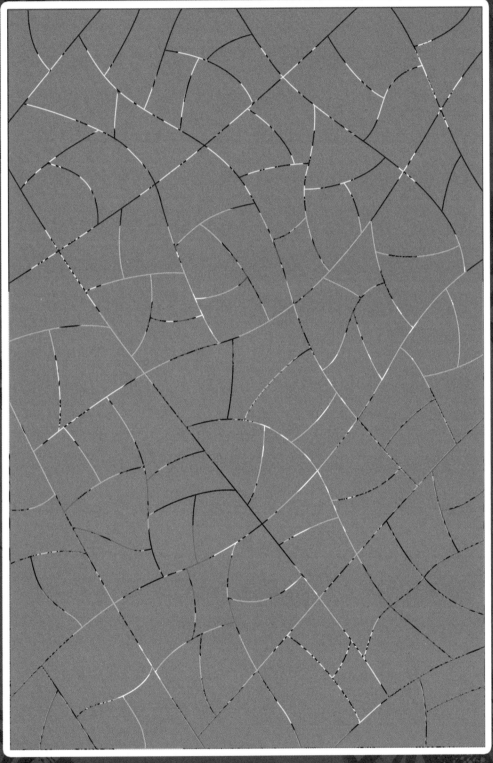

AMAZING FANTASY #15
(AUGUST 1962)
ART BY JACK KIRBY (PENCILS),
STEVE DITKO (INKS)

THE INCREDIBLE HULK

AT THE HEIGHT OF THE COLD WAR, DOCTOR BRUCE BANNER IS HARD AT WORK DEVELOPING A *TERRIBLE NEW WEAPON* FOR THE UNITED STATES--THE DREADED *GAMMA BOMB*. HARNESSING THE UNPREDICTABLE, POTENTIALLY DEVASTATING POWER OF GAMMA RAYS, THE BOMB IS SURE TO HELP THE AMERICANS IN THEIR STRUGGLE AGAINST THE SOVIET UNION. BUT UNKNOWN TO BANNER, A SOVIET SPY IS SECRETLY PART OF HIS TEAM.

WHEN THE DAY OF THE TEST ARRIVES, A TEENAGER NAMED RICK JONES DRIVES OUT ONTO THE TESTING GROUND ON A DARE FROM HIS FRIENDS. BANNER SEES THE YOUTH AND ORDERS THE COUNTDOWN PAUSED SO HE CAN GET THE TEENAGER OUT OF HARM'S WAY. BUT THE SPY HAS OTHER PLANS AND *RESUMES THE COUNTDOWN*. BANNER IS ABLE TO GET JONES TO SAFETY BUT IS CAUGHT IN THE FULL FURY OF THE *EXPLODING GAMMA BOMB*.

MIRACULOUSLY, BANNER SURVIVES. ONLY LATER DO THE EFFECTS OF THE GAMMA BOMB BECOME KNOWN. AS NIGHT FALLS, BANNER FINDS HIMSELF TRANSFORMED INTO A *HUGE, BRUTISH NIGHTMARE OF A MAN* THE MILITARY SOON DUBS *THE HULK*. THE HULK AND JONES ARE THEN CAPTURED BY ANOTHER SOVIET AGENT KNOWN AS THE GARGOYLE AND *TAKEN TO THE USSR*.

BUT WHEN HE ARRIVES, NIGHT HAS TURNED TO DAY, AND THE HULK CHANGES BACK TO BANNER. USING HIS *KNOWLEDGE OF RADIATION*, HE HELPS THE DISFIGURED GARGOYLE ACHIEVE HIS WISH OF BECOMING A "NORMAL" MAN. BANNER AND JONES RETURN TO THE U.S., AS THE SCIENTIST AWAITS THE COMING OF NIGHT.

I AM THE HULK!

NOTHING CAN HARM ME!! NOTHING CAN BEAT ME!!

TALES TO ASTONISH
THE INCREDIBLE
HULK
AND THE SUB-MARINER

WHERE WALK THE IMMORTALS!

IN HIS FIRST APPEARANCE, THE HULK WAS *GRAY IN COLOR*. BUT ACCORDING TO STAN LEE, THE EFFECT WASN'T CONSISTENT THROUGHOUT THE ISSUE. IN ONE PANEL, HE EVEN APPEARED TO BE GREEN! THAT COLOR STUCK, AND WITH *THE INCREDIBLE HULK #2* (JULY 1962), THE CHARACTER WAS GREEN.

THE FIRST ISSUE OF *THE HULK* ALSO INTRODUCED BETTY ROSS, DAUGHTER OF GENERAL THADDEUS "THUNDERBOLT" ROSS, WHO WOULD GO ON TO MARRY BRUCE BANNER IN *THE INCREDIBLE HULK #319* (MAY 1986).

AS HULK, BANNER WAS A FOUNDING MEMBER OF *THE AVENGERS*. HE LEFT THE TEAM SHORTLY AFTER THEIR BATTLES WITH *LOKI* AND *THE SPACE PHANTOM* TO TEAM UP WITH THE SUB-MARINER AGAINST THEM!

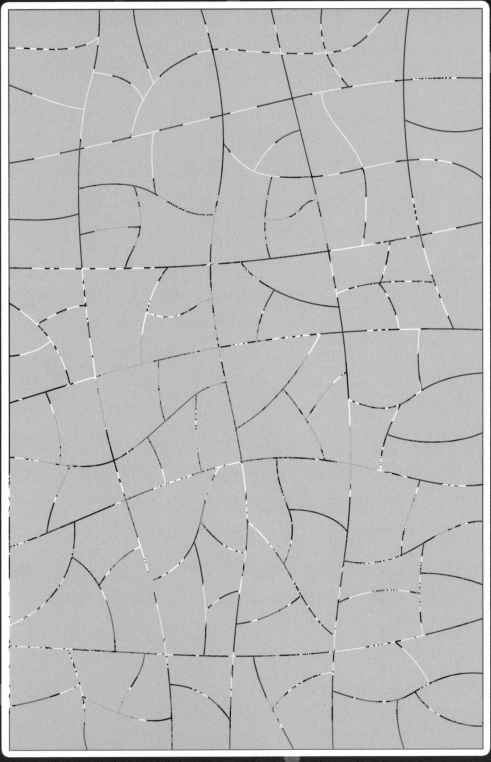

THE INCREDIBLE HULK #1
(MAY 1962)
ART BY JACK KIRBY (PENCILS),
GEORGE ROUSSOS (INKS)

BLACK PANTHER

STAN LEE AND JACK KIRBY INTRODUCED A STAGGERING NUMBER OF CHARACTERS AND CONCEPTS IN THEIR FANTASTIC FOUR STORIES. AMONG THEM ARE THE SILVER SURFER, THE INHUMANS, AND GALACTUS, THE DEVOURER OF WORLDS. BUT ONE OF THEIR *GREATEST CREATIONS* ARRIVED IN THE PAGES OF *FANTASTIC FOUR #52* (JULY 1966): T'CHALLA, *THE BLACK PANTHER.* WHEN THE FANTASTIC FOUR RECEIVE A WONDROUS, TECHNOLOGICALLY ADVANCED FLYING CRAFT AND AN INVITATION TO VISIT THE *MYSTERIOUS AFRICAN NATION OF WAKANDA*, REED RICHARDS AND HIS TEAMMATES ARE INTRIGUED. THEY EAGERLY ACCEPT AND TRAVEL ACROSS THE ATLANTIC OCEAN TO MEET THEIR HOST.

UPON THEIR ARRIVAL, THE FANTASTIC FOUR FIND THEMSELVES IN A FOREST *UNLIKE ANY OTHER*, ENTIRELY MECHANICAL IN NATURE. WHEN THEY LEAVE THEIR SHIP, THE TEAM IS IMMEDIATELY BESIEGED BY THE BLACK PANTHER AND HIS GUARDS. THEY FACE *DANGEROUS TRAPS* AS WELL AS THEIR APPARENT ENEMIES; SEPARATED, THE FANTASTIC FOUR ARE *OVERWHELMED.*

BUT THE TEAM MANAGES TO REGROUP. FIGHTING AS A *COHESIVE UNIT*, THEY PROVE MORE THAN A MATCH FOR T'CHALLA AND HIS WARRIORS. SURPRISINGLY, T'CHALLA CALLS OFF THE ATTACK AND ANNOUNCES THAT HE WAS ONLY TESTING THE *FIGHTING PROWESS* AND *POWERS* OF THE FANTASTIC FOUR. HE HAS ASKED THEM TO COME TO WAKANDA BECAUSE HE NEEDS THEIR HELP! ALAS, READERS WOULD HAVE TO WAIT TO *ISSUE #53* TO FIND OUT WHY...

OKAY, WE CAN'T LEAVE YOU HANGING. IN *FANTASTIC FOUR #53*, IT'S REVEALED THAT T'CHALLA NEEDS THE FANTASTIC FOUR'S HELP TO DEFEAT ULYSSES KLAW, AN EXPLORER WHO CAME TO WAKANDA TO STEAL THE RARE METAL *VIBRANIUM* AND KILLED T'CHALLA'S FATHER, KING T'CHAKA.

VIBRANIUM WAS ONE OF THE ELEMENTS USED BY METALLURGIST DOCTOR MYRON MACLAIN TO CREATE *CAPTAIN AMERICA'S SHIELD.* THE PROCESS HAS NEVER BEEN DUPLICATED, MAKING CAP'S SHIELD TRULY ONE OF A KIND.

NOT ONLY WAS T'CHALLA THE RULER OF AN ENTIRE COUNTRY, BUT HE ALSO JOINED *EARTH'S MIGHTIEST HEROES* IN *THE AVENGERS #52* (MAY 1968) FOLLOWING HIS EFFORTS TO SAVE THE TEAM FROM THE MURDEROUS GRIM REAPER.

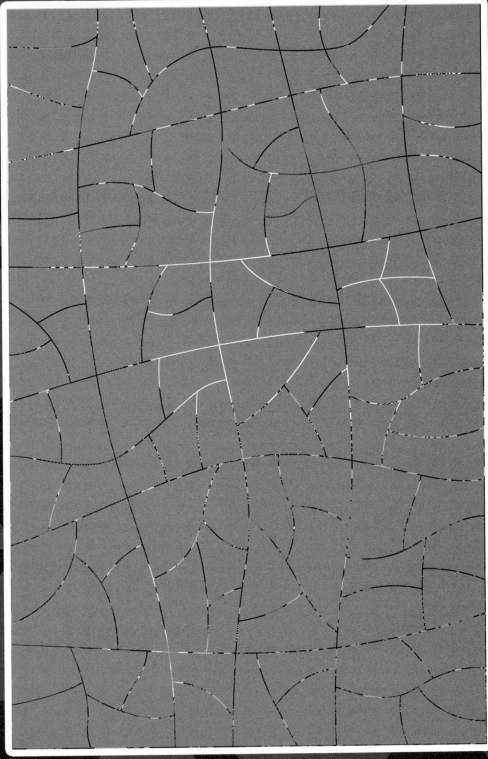

FANTASTIC FOUR #52
(JULY 1966)
ART BY JACK KIRBY (PENCILS),
JOE SINNOTT (INKS)

CAPTAIN AMERICA

AS WORLD WAR II LOOMED ON THE HORIZON, FRAIL STEVE ROGERS WAS DESPERATE TO SERVE HIS COUNTRY. REJECTED FOR SERVICE, ROGERS WAS FINALLY SELECTED FOR A *TOP-SECRET EXPERIMENT.* GIVEN THE SUPER-SOLDIER SERUM AND EXPOSED TO MYSTERIOUS VITA-RAYS, ROGERS BECAME *CAPTAIN AMERICA*--THE LIVING LEGEND OF WORLD WAR II!

FOLLOWING HIS WAR-TIME EXPLOITS, CAPTAIN AMERICA RETURNED IN *THE AVENGERS #4* AND WAS SOON GIVEN HIS OWN SERIES IN A BOOK SHARED WITH *IRON MAN* CALLED *TALES OF SUSPENSE.* FROM ISSUE #59 (NOVEMBER 1964) THROUGH ISSUE #99 (MARCH 1968), CAP ENCOUNTERED FOES BOTH OLD AND NEW.

BUT IN APRIL OF 1968, THE STAR-SPANGLED AVENGER WAS FINALLY GIVEN HIS OWN SERIES. WITH *CAPTAIN AMERICA #100*, READERS WERE TREATED TO AN ALL-NEW RETELLING OF CAP'S AWESOME ORIGINS. AND THAT WAS JUST IN THE *FIRST THREE PAGES!* THEN IT WAS BACK TO BUSINESS, AS THE BLACK PANTHER JOINED THE ACTION TO TAKE DOWN CAP'S OLD FOE, BARON ZEMO.

WITH THE HELP OF S.H.I.E.L.D. AGENT SHARON CARTER, THE HEROES FOIL ZEMO'S PLANS, ULTIMATELY REVEALING THAT "ZEMO" WASN'T ZEMO AT ALL--BUT THE VILLAIN'S PERSONAL PILOT. THE REAL ZEMO HAD PERISHED YEARS AGO. AT THE CLOSE OF THE ADVENTURE, CAPTAIN AMERICA SUGGESTED THAT THE BLACK PANTHER CONSIDER JOINING THE AVENGERS.

THE AVENGERS #52, THE ISSUE WHERE T'CHALLA JOINS THE TEAM, APPEARED ON NEWSSTANDS ONE MONTH AFTER *CAPTAIN AMERICA #100!*

CAPTAIN AMERICA HAD A PARTNER IN WORLD WAR II NAMED *BUCKY BARNES,* WHO WAS THOUGHT TO BE KILLED. CAP WOULDN'T HAVE ANOTHER PARTNER UNTIL HE TEAMED UP WITH THE FALCON IN *CAPTAIN AMERICA #133* (JANUARY 1971).

DECADES LATER, IT WOULD BE REVEALED THAT *BUCKY BARNES* HAD SURVIVED WORLD WAR II AND WAS OPERATING AS AN ASSASSIN CODE-NAMED *THE WINTER SOLDIER.*

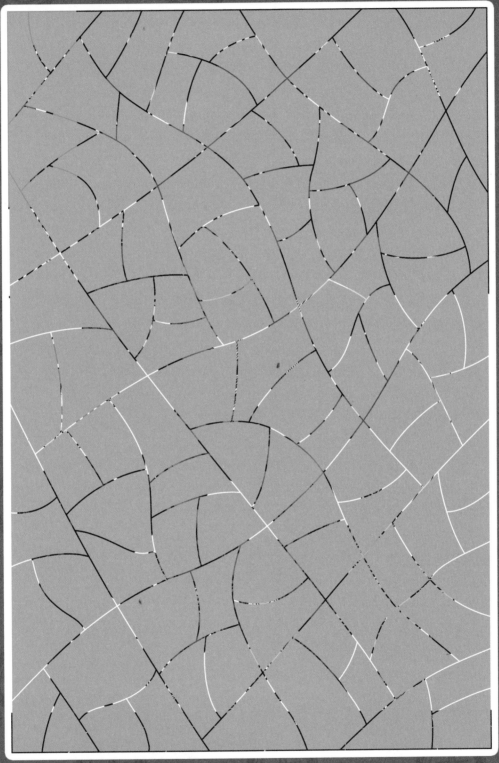

CAPTAIN AMERICA #100
(APRIL 1968)
ART BY JACK KIRBY (PENCILS),
SYD SHORES (INKS),
SAM ROSEN (LETTERS)

BLACK WIDOW

WHEN NATASHA ROMANOFF, A.K.A. THE BLACK WIDOW, MADE HER FIRST APPEARANCE IN *TALES OF SUSPENSE #52* (APRIL 1964), IT WASN'T AS A SUPER HERO! AN ENEMY SPY, THE BLACK WIDOW TRAVELED TO THE U.S. UNDER THE GUISE OF "MADAME NATASHA," A TEACHER FROM UKRAINE WHO WISHED TO OBSERVE TONY STARK'S TECHNOLOGY UP CLOSE. HER PURPOSE WAS MORE NEFARIOUS--ELIMINATE STARK AND HIS BODYGUARD IRON MAN!

HER PLAN UNRAVELED, AND THE BLACK WIDOW *FLED INTO THE SHADOWS.* SHE WOULD REAPPEAR TO BEDEVIL STARK AGAIN BEFORE FINALLY CHANGING HER WAYS AND USING HER ESPIONAGE AND FIGHTING SKILLS ON THE *SIDE OF RIGHT.*

THE BLACK WIDOW WOULD GO ON TO FIGHT ALONGSIDE THE AVENGERS, INCLUDING HER FORMER NEMESIS, IRON MAN. EVENTUALLY, SHE WOULD LEAVE THE TEAM TO STRIKE OUT ON HER OWN. ONE OF HER FIRST *POST-AVENGERS ENCOUNTERS* INVOLVED SPIDER-MAN. SEEKING TO DISCOVER THE SECRET OF SPIDER-MAN'S *ARACHNID ABILITIES* AND ADD THOSE POWERS TO HER OWN, THE BLACK WIDOW CONFRONTED THE WALL-CRAWLER.

WITH *AMAZING ADVENTURES #1* (AUGUST 1970), BLACK WIDOW WOULD EMBARK ON HER FIRST-EVER *SOLO ADVENTURE.* NOW LIVING IN A LUXURIOUS MANHATTAN PENTHOUSE APARTMENT, NATASHA HAD GROWN BORED. SHE CRAVED THE DANGER OF HER EARLIER LIFE AS A SPY. WHEN SHE LEARNED THAT HER HOUSEKEEPER'S SON HAD RUN AFOUL OF LOAN SHARKS, NATASHA DONNED A *SLEEK NEW COSTUME* AND WRIST-MOUNTED "WIDOW'S BITES." IT WAS TIME FOR BLACK WIDOW TO LEAP INTO ACTION. EASILY DEFEATING THE CRIMINALS AND RESCUING THE SON, BLACK WIDOW WAS NOW FIRMLY ON THE SIDE OF RIGHT.

*T*HE BLACK WIDOW OFFICIALLY JOINED THE AVENGERS IN ISSUE #111 (MAY 1973) OF THAT SERIES, FOLLOWING AN ADVENTURE THAT SAW HER DOING BATTLE AGAINST THE ARCH-VILLAIN *MAGNETO.*

THE *BIGGER* THEY ARE, THE *HARDER* THEY FALL!

*W*HEN HAWKEYE FIRST APPEARED IN *TALES OF SUSPENSE #57* (SEPTEMBER 1964), HE TEAMED UP WITH THE BLACK WIDOW AS PART OF HER ELABORATE PLAN TO EXACT REVENGE ON TONY STARK AND IRON MAN.

*T*HE BLACK WIDOW ALSO PARTNERED WITH *DAREDEVIL* FOR A RUN OF THAT HERO'S BOOK, DURING WHICH THE TITLE WAS CHANGED TO *DAREDEVIL AND THE BLACK WIDOW* (ISSUES #93-#108).

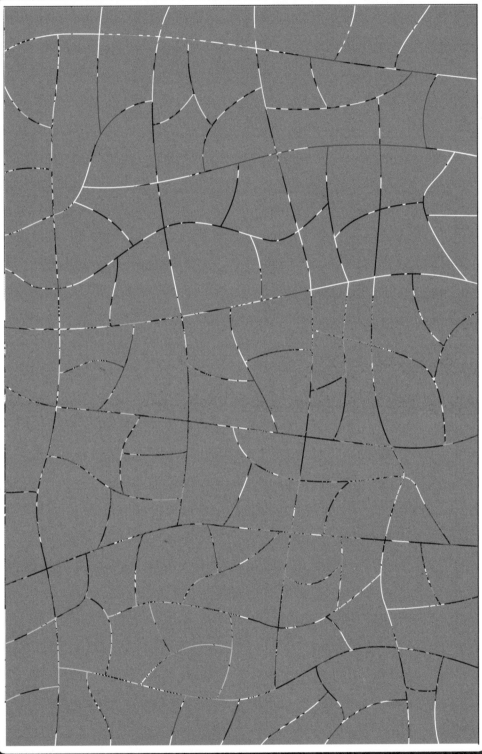

AMAZING ADVENTURES
VOLUME 2, #1
(AUGUST 1970)
BLACK WIDOW ART BY
JOHN ROMITA, SR.
INHUMANS ART BY JACK KIRBY

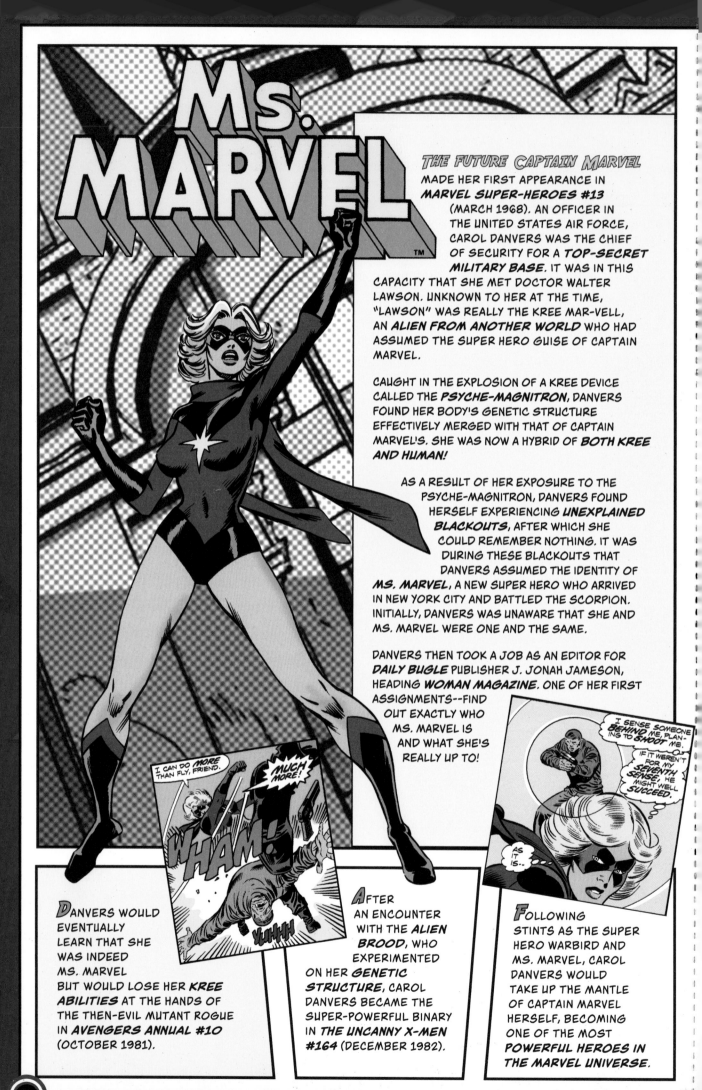

MS. MARVEL

THE FUTURE CAPTAIN MARVEL MADE HER FIRST APPEARANCE IN *MARVEL SUPER-HEROES #13* (MARCH 1968). AN OFFICER IN THE UNITED STATES AIR FORCE, CAROL DANVERS WAS THE CHIEF OF SECURITY FOR A *TOP-SECRET MILITARY BASE*. IT WAS IN THIS CAPACITY THAT SHE MET DOCTOR WALTER LAWSON. UNKNOWN TO HER AT THE TIME, "LAWSON" WAS REALLY THE KREE MAR-VELL, AN *ALIEN FROM ANOTHER WORLD* WHO HAD ASSUMED THE SUPER HERO GUISE OF CAPTAIN MARVEL.

CAUGHT IN THE EXPLOSION OF A KREE DEVICE CALLED THE *PSYCHE-MAGNITRON*, DANVERS FOUND HER BODY'S GENETIC STRUCTURE EFFECTIVELY MERGED WITH THAT OF CAPTAIN MARVEL'S. SHE WAS NOW A HYBRID OF *BOTH KREE AND HUMAN!*

AS A RESULT OF HER EXPOSURE TO THE PSYCHE-MAGNITRON, DANVERS FOUND HERSELF EXPERIENCING *UNEXPLAINED BLACKOUTS*, AFTER WHICH SHE COULD REMEMBER NOTHING. IT WAS DURING THESE BLACKOUTS THAT DANVERS ASSUMED THE IDENTITY OF *MS. MARVEL*, A NEW SUPER HERO WHO ARRIVED IN NEW YORK CITY AND BATTLED THE SCORPION. INITIALLY, DANVERS WAS UNAWARE THAT SHE AND MS. MARVEL WERE ONE AND THE SAME.

DANVERS THEN TOOK A JOB AS AN EDITOR FOR *DAILY BUGLE* PUBLISHER J. JONAH JAMESON, HEADING *WOMAN MAGAZINE*. ONE OF HER FIRST ASSIGNMENTS--FIND OUT EXACTLY WHO MS. MARVEL IS AND WHAT SHE'S REALLY UP TO!

I CAN DO *MORE* THAN FLY, FRIEND.

MUCH MORE!

WHAM!

YUHHH

I SENSE SOMEONE *BEHIND* ME, PLAN-ING TO *SHOOT* ME.

IF IT WEREN'T FOR MY *SEVENTH SENSE*, HE MIGHT WELL *SUCCEED.*

AS IT IS...

DANVERS WOULD EVENTUALLY LEARN THAT SHE WAS INDEED MS. MARVEL BUT WOULD LOSE HER *KREE ABILITIES* AT THE HANDS OF THE THEN-EVIL MUTANT ROGUE IN *AVENGERS ANNUAL #10* (OCTOBER 1981).

AFTER AN ENCOUNTER WITH THE *ALIEN BROOD*, WHO EXPERIMENTED ON HER *GENETIC STRUCTURE*, CAROL DANVERS BECAME THE SUPER-POWERFUL BINARY IN *THE UNCANNY X-MEN #164* (DECEMBER 1982).

FOLLOWING STINTS AS THE SUPER HERO WARBIRD AND MS. MARVEL, CAROL DANVERS WOULD TAKE UP THE MANTLE OF CAPTAIN MARVEL HERSELF, BECOMING ONE OF THE MOST *POWERFUL HEROES IN THE MARVEL UNIVERSE.*

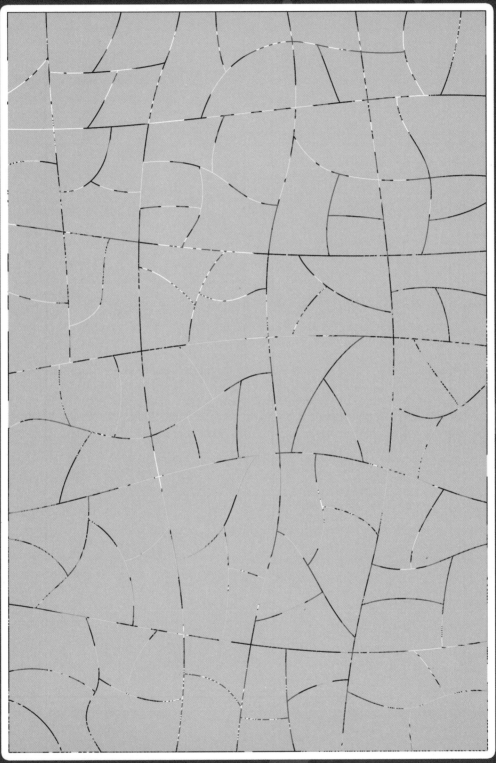

MS. MARVEL #1
(JANUARY 1977)
ART BY JOHN ROMITA, SR.

THE SAVAGE SHE-HULK

IF YOU EVER WONDERED

WHAT IT WOULD BE LIKE BEING RELATED TO *THE INCREDIBLE HULK*, WONDER NO MORE! WHEN A DESPERATE BRUCE BANNER ARRIVES IN LOS ANGELES, HE'S AT THE *END OF HIS ROPE* AND TIRED OF RUNNING ALL THE TIME AS A RESULT OF HIS ACTIVITIES AS THE HULK. HE CONTACTS HIS COUSIN JENNIFER WALTERS, A SUCCESSFUL LAWYER.

WALTERS TELLS HER COUSIN ABOUT THE CASE IN WHICH SHE'S CURRENTLY INVOLVED, DEFENDING A CRIMINAL NAMED MONKTON WHO HAS BEEN ACCUSED OF *KILLING THE BODYGUARD* OF ANOTHER CRIMINAL, NICK TRASK. WALTERS BELIEVES THAT MONKTON WAS *FRAMED BY TRASK*, WHO KILLED THE BODYGUARD HIMSELF.

WALTERS AND BANNER DRIVE TO HER HOUSE AND SHE IS *AMBUSHED* BY TRASK'S THUGS, WHO DELIVER AN ALMOST SURELY MORTAL BULLET WOUND. RUSHING HER INSIDE THE HOUSE, BANNER PERFORMS AN *EMERGENCY TRANSFUSION* ON HIS COUSIN, USING HIS OWN GAMMA-IRRADIATED BLOOD.

SURVIVING THE ATTACK, WALTERS AWAKENS IN THE HOSPITAL, ONLY TO FIND TRASK'S THUGS MAKING ANOTHER ATTEMPT ON HER LIFE. EXCEPT THIS TIME, SHE TRANSFORMS INTO A GREEN GIANT KNOWN AS *THE SHE-HULK*! SHE MAKES SHORT WORK OF HER ATTACKERS AND VOWS THAT FROM NOW ON, WHATEVER JENNIFER WALTERS CAN'T HANDLE, THE SHE-HULK WILL.

UNLIKE HER COUSIN, JENNIFER WALTERS RETAINED HER INTELLECT WHENEVER SHE TRANSFORMED INTO THE SHE-HULK.

SHE-HULK HAD THE AMAZING DISTINCTION OF BELONGING TO BOTH THE FANTASTIC FOUR AND THE AVENGERS AT THE SAME TIME! WHEN SHE FOUND TIME TO PRACTICE LAW AND SLEEP IS ANYONE'S GUESS!

ALTHOUGH WALTERS USED TO PRACTICE LAW IN HER SHE-HULK FORM, THESE DAYS HER SAVAGE SIDE HAS TAKEN OVER.

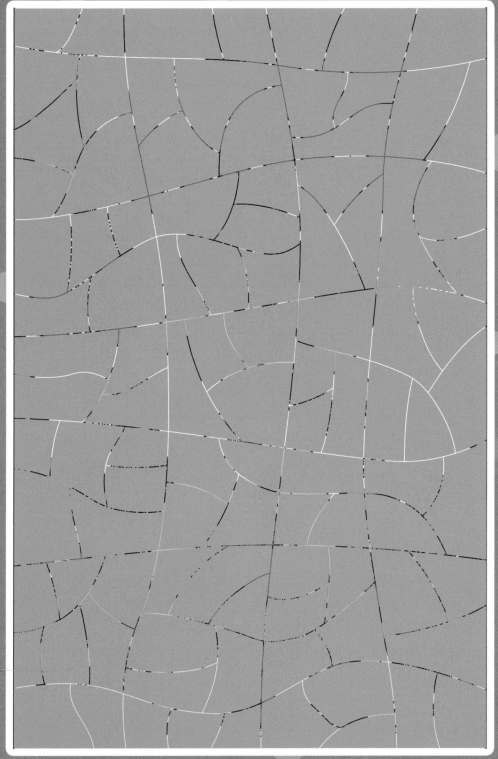

THE SAVAGE SHE-HULK
(FEBRUARY 1980)
ART BY JOHN BUSCEMA (PENCILS),
IRV WATANABE (LETTERS)

THE Fantastic Four

ARRIVED WITH THE FIRST APPEARANCE OF THE FANTASTIC FOUR IN, APPROPRIATELY ENOUGH, *FANTASTIC FOUR #1* (NOVEMBER 1961). AS THE STORY UNFOLDED, READERS WERE INTRODUCED TO *FOUR UNLIKELY HEROES*--WHO DID NOT WEAR COSTUMES--AS THEY CAME TOGETHER TO FACE A DIRE THREAT TO HUMANITY.

SUE STORM (A.K.A. INVISIBLE GIRL), BEN GRIMM (A.K.A. THE THING), SUE'S BROTHER JOHNNY STORM (A.K.A. HUMAN TORCH), AND REED RICHARDS (A.K.A. MR. FANTASTIC) RECOUNTED HOW THEY RECEIVED THEIR *INCREDIBLE POWERS* FOLLOWING THE TEST FLIGHT OF A SPACECRAFT DESIGNED BY RICHARDS. ON ITS MAIDEN VOYAGE, THE SHIP WAS BOMBARDED BY *COSMIC RAYS*, FORCING THE CREW TO CRASH LAND. THEY SURVIVED, BUT THE UNPREDICTABLE COSMIC RAYS HAD GIVEN EACH A *FANTASTIC NEW ABILITY*.

COMING TOGETHER AS *THE FANTASTIC FOUR*, THE INTREPID ADVENTURERS SET OUT TO FIND WHO (OR WHAT) WAS BEHIND THE MYSTERIOUS CAVE-INS THAT WERE CONSUMING ATOMIC POWER PLANTS AROUND THE GLOBE. THEIR SEARCH LED THEM TO MONSTER ISLE, THE HOME OF THE MALEVOLENT MOLE MAN. WITH AN *ARMY OF MONSTROUS CREATURES* AT HIS COMMAND, THE MOLE MAN PLANNED TO INVADE THE SURFACE WORLD.

THANKS TO THE *COMBINED MIGHT* OF THE FANTASTIC FOUR, THE MOLE MAN'S SINISTER SCHEME WAS FOILED, AND THE ENTRANCE TO THE SUBTERRANEAN WORLD OF MONSTERS WAS SEALED. BUT FOR HOW LONG?

*T*HE FANTASTIC FOUR WOULDN'T RECEIVE THE FAMILIAR BLUE COSTUMES WITH THE NUMBER FOUR UNTIL *FANTASTIC FOUR #3* (MARCH 1962).

*T*HE FANTASTIC FOUR'S *ARCHENEMY*, DOCTOR DOOM, WAS REED RICHARDS' COLLEGE ROOMMATE! DOOM ATTENDED STATE UNIVERSITY WITH BOTH RICHARDS AND BEN GRIMM.

*W*HILE THE THING WAS OFF WORLD FOLLOWING THE EVENTS OF MARVEL SUPER HEROES SECRET WARS, THE *SENSATIONAL SHE-HULK* TOOK BEN GRIMM'S PLACE ON THE TEAM IN *FANTASTIC FOUR #265* (APRIL 1984).

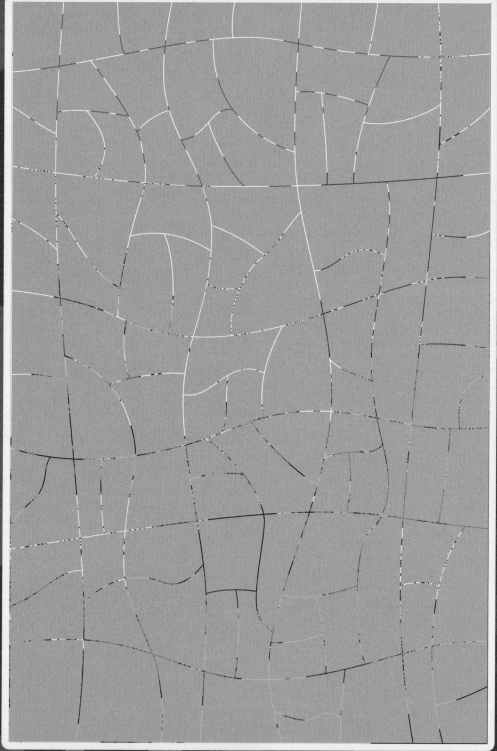

FANTASTIC FOUR #1
(NOVEMBER 1961)
ART BY JACK KIRBY (PENCILS),
DICK AYERS (INKS)

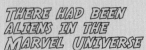

GUARDIANS OF THE GALAXY

THERE HAD BEEN ALIENS IN THE MARVEL UNIVERSE ALMOST SINCE THE BEGINNING. THE SHAPE-CHANGING SKRULLS MADE THEIR FIRST APPEARANCE IN *THE FANTASTIC FOUR #2* (JANUARY 1962), AND THE WARLIKE KREE ARRIVED IN *MARVEL SUPER-HEROES #12* (DECEMBER 1967). BUT THE WORLD WAS COMPLETELY UNPREPARED FOR THE TEAM THAT WOULD SOON ARRIVE ON THE SCENE.

HAILING FROM THE PLANET JUPITER, CHARLIE-27 HAS BEEN ON A MISSION FOR THE LAST SIX MONTHS. WHEN HE RETURNS HOME, HE DISCOVERS THAT A RACE OF *SINISTER ALIENS* KNOWN AS *THE BADOON* HAVE TAKEN OVER. UNABLE TO TAKE THEM DOWN ON HIS OWN, CHARLIE-27 LEAVES JUPITER AND TRAVELS THROUGHOUT THE GALAXY TO ASSEMBLE A TEAM WHO CAN.

ALONG THE WAY, HE RECRUITS MARTINEX ON THE PLANET PLUTO. THE PAIR NEXT ARRIVES ON EARTH, WHERE THEY ATTEMPT TO ENLIST THE AID OF VANCE ASTRO AND A CENTAURIAN NAMED YONDU, WHO ARE THEMSELVES ON THE RUN FROM THE BADOON.

OF COURSE, A CASE OF MISTAKEN IDENTITY ENSUES, AS ASTRO AND YONDU BELIEVE THAT CHARLIE-27 AND MARTINEX ARE ACTUALLY BADOON. THE FOUR HEROES FIGHT BRIEFLY, UNTIL THEY REALIZE THEIR ERROR. AS THEY COME TO REALIZE THAT *THEY'RE ALL AGAINST THE BADOON*, THE FOUR BEINGS POOL THEIR POWERS AND ABILITIES TOGETHER, FORMING *THE GUARDIANS OF THE GALAXY*.

THE GUARDIANS WOULD NEXT APPEAR IN *MARVEL TWO-IN-ONE #5* (SEPTEMBER 1974), WHERE THEY TEAMED UP WITH THE FANTASTIC FOUR'S THING AND CAPTAIN AMERICA TO *FIGHT THE BADOON*.

BELIEVE IT OR NOT, THESE GUARDIANS OF THE GALAXY HAILED FROM THE *DISTANT 30TH CENTURY!* THEY ENCOUNTERED CAPTAIN AMERICA AND THE THING COURTESY OF *DOCTOR DOOM'S TIME MACHINE.*

IN 2008, A NEW TEAM THAT INCLUDED STAR-LORD, GAMORA, DRAX THE DESTROYER, ROCKET, AND GROOT APPEARED IN *ANNIHILATION: CONQUEST #6* (APRIL 2008). THEY WOULD OFFICIALLY BECOME THE GUARDIANS IN *GUARDIANS OF THE GALAXY #1* (JULY 2008).

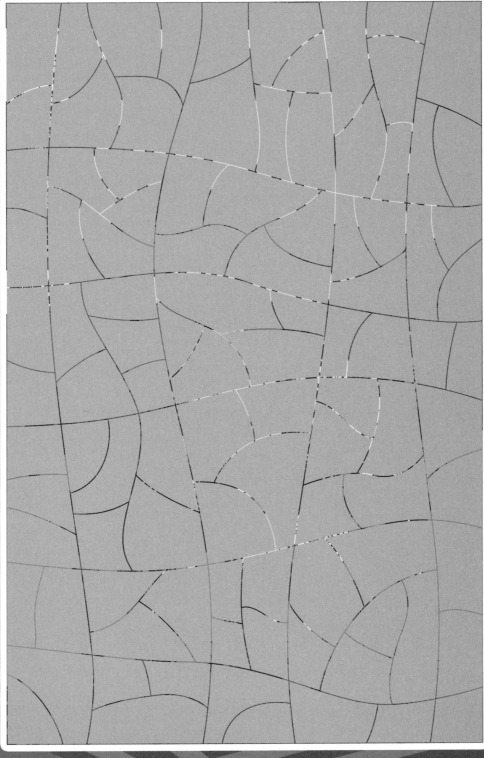

MARVEL SUPER-HEROES #18
(JANUARY 1969)
ART BY GENE COLAN

THE AVENGERS

IF IT WEREN'T FOR THOR'S ADOPTED BROTHER LOKI, THEN THE AVENGERS WOULD HAVE NEVER COME TO BE! BUT WE'RE GETTING AHEAD OF OURSELVES. FOLLOWING AN EARLIER ESCAPADE, LOKI WAS IMPRISONED ON THE *ISLE OF SILENCE* ON ASGARD. SCHEMING REVENGE AGAINST HIS HATED BROTHER, LOKI USES THE MISUNDERSTOOD HULK TO LURE DOCTOR DONALD BLAKE INTO TAKING ACTION AS THOR. HE CASTS AN ILLUSION THAT *LIVE DYNAMITE* APPEAR ON A BRIDGE IN FRONT OF AN ONCOMING TRAIN. IN AN ATTEMPT TO SAVE THE TRAIN, HULK DIVES FOR THE DYNAMITE. BUT THE "DYNAMITE" DISAPPEARS, AND HULK DESTROYS THE BRIDGE BY ACCIDENT (THOUGH HE DOES SAVE THE TRAIN).

UNFORTUNATELY FOR LOKI, THOR ISN'T THE ONLY SUPER HERO TO TAKE NOTICE. IN AN EFFORT TO HELP HIS FRIEND HULK, RICK JONES SENDS A MESSAGE TO THE FANTASTIC FOUR. LOKI REROUTES THE MESSAGE, WHERE IT'S INADVERTENTLY INTERCEPTED BY IRON MAN, ANT-MAN AND THE WASP, AND THOR. *THE HEROES MEET,* REALIZE WHAT'S HAPPENED, AND FORM A *BATTLE PLAN.* WHILE THOR CONFRONTS LOKI IN ASGARD, THE OTHERS TACKLE HULK, WHO HAS TAKEN REFUGE IN A CIRCUS.

IN ASGARD, THOR BATTLES LOKI, WHO HAS MADE A *TERRIBLE BARGAIN* WITH THE UNDERGROUND TROLLS--IF THEY OBEYED LOKI, HE PROMISED THEM THAT THOR WOULD BE THEIR SLAVE FOREVER. THOR BESTED THE TROLLS AND LOKI, TAKING HIS BROTHER BACK TO EARTH TO FACE THE *WRATH OF THE HEROES* AND A VERY ANGRY HULK.

A LAST-DITCH EFFORT BY LOKI TO *ATTACK THE HEROES* WAS FOILED BY ANT-MAN AND HIS ANTS, WHO SUCCEEDED IN CONTAINING THE TRICKSTER. BEFORE LEAVING, ANT-MAN AND THE WASP SUGGESTED THE HEROES COMBINE THEIR EFFORTS, AND THUS *THE AVENGERS* CAME TO BE.

THE AVENGERS TOOK UP RESIDENCE IN A *MANSION* OWNED BY TONY STARK. AT THE TIME, NONE OF THE MEMBERS WAS AWARE THAT STARK WAS SECRETLY *IRON MAN!*

FOLLOWING THE DEPARTURE OF THE HULK IN *THE AVENGERS #2* (NOVEMBER 1963), THE TEAM WAS ONE PERSON SHORT UNTIL THEY DISCOVERED THE FROZEN *CAPTAIN AMERICA,* WHO JOINED THEIR RANKS IN *THE AVENGERS #4* (MARCH 1964).

THE ORIGINAL AVENGERS LEFT THE TEAM IN *THE AVENGERS #16* (MAY 1965). ONLY CAPTAIN AMERICA REMAINED, AND --- HE RECRUITED *THREE NEW MEMBERS:* ACE ARCHER HAWKEYE, SPEEDSTER QUICKSILVER, AND HIS SISTER, THE POWERFUL SCARLET WITCH.

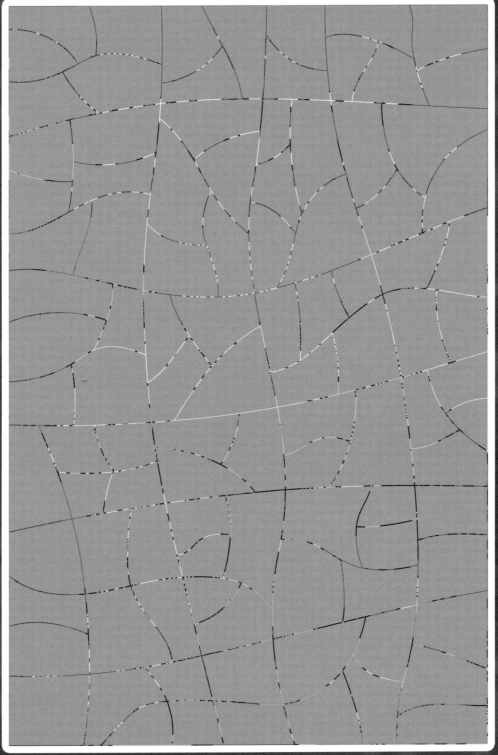

THE AVENGERS #1
(SEPTEMBER 1963)
ART BY JACK KIRBY (PENCILS),
DICK AYERS (INKS)

SOLUTIONS

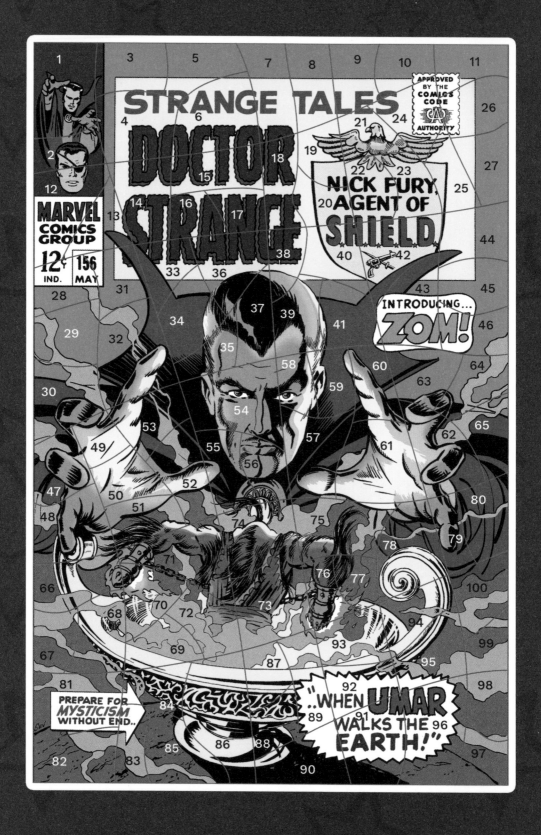

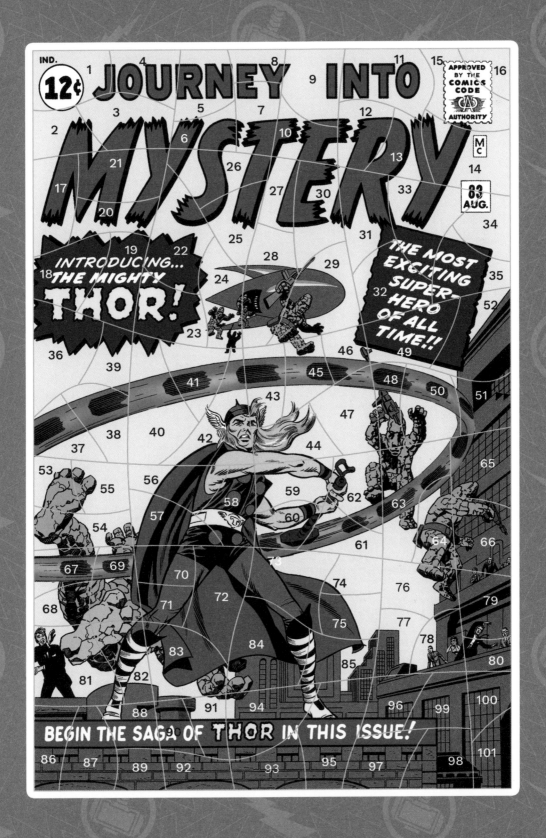

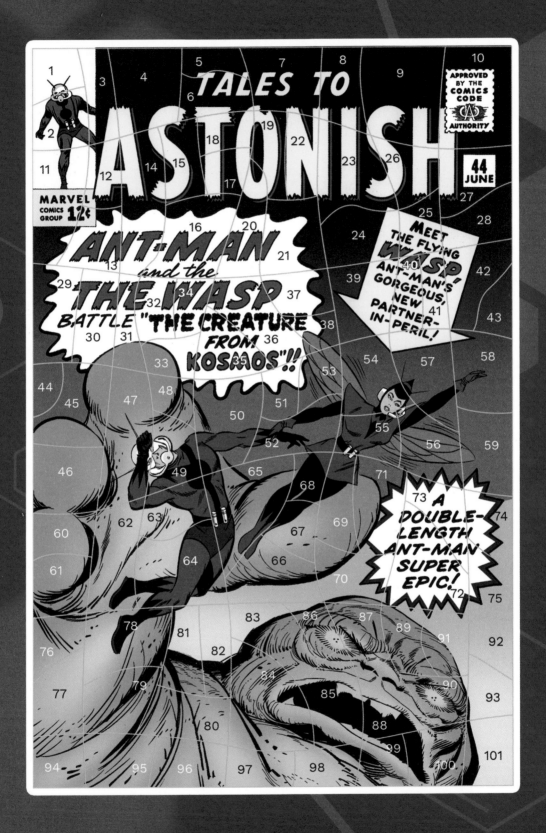

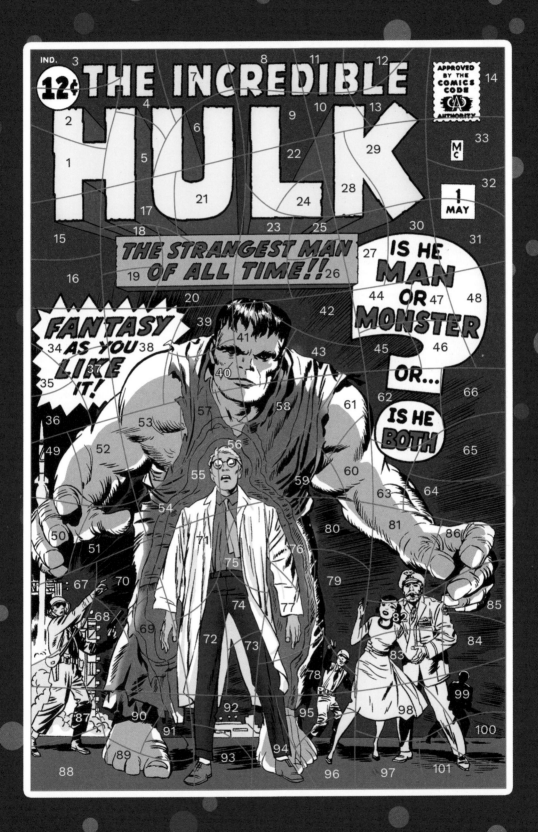

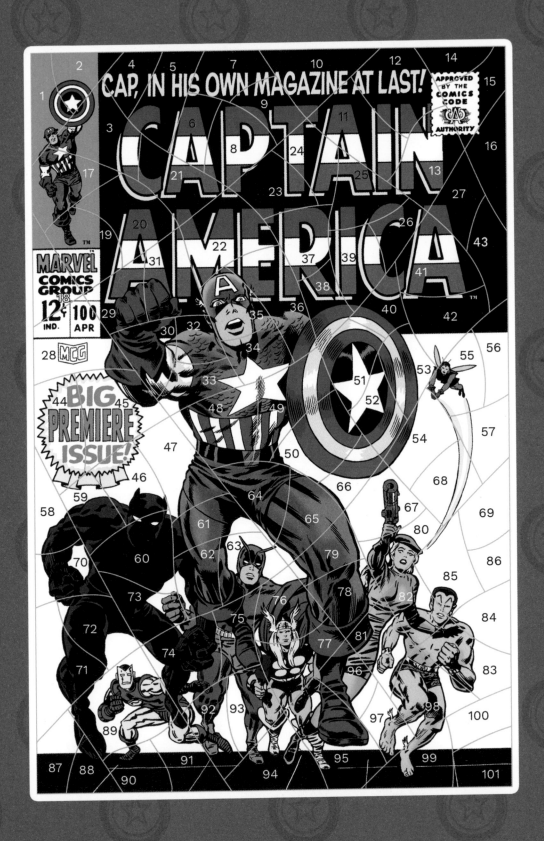

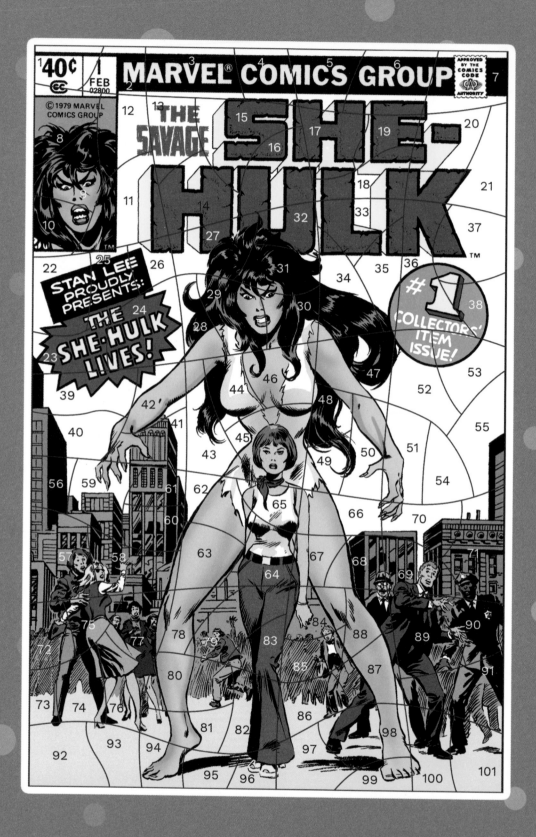

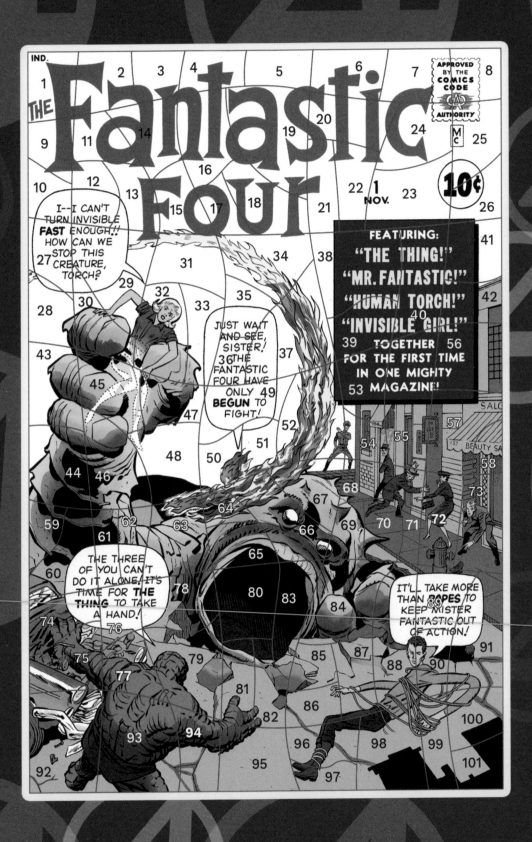

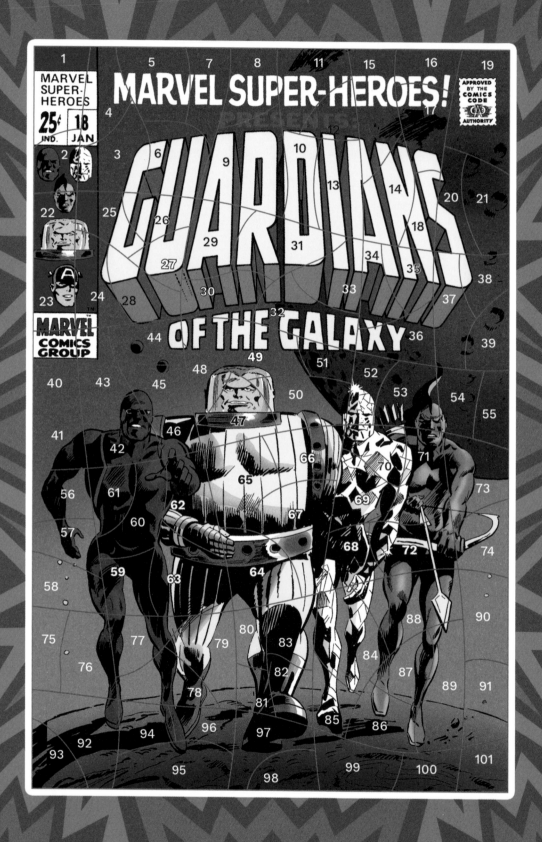

Ms. MAR
30¢
THIS FEMA
FIGHTS BA
MARVEL
COMIC
APPROVED BY THE COMICS CODE AUTHORITY
ALL-OUT
FABULO
FIRS
ISSU
T LAST!
AT LAST
A BOLD NE
SUPER-HERO
IN THE
SENSES-ST
TRADITI
FEATURING THE
MYSTERIOUS W
WARRIOR SINCE
MEDUSA! AND, IF
THINK OUR LEADIN
SOMETHING, W
YOU SEE HER STA
SUPPORTING
STAR-STUDDED
NG CAST!
SENSES
TRADIT
SPIDER-

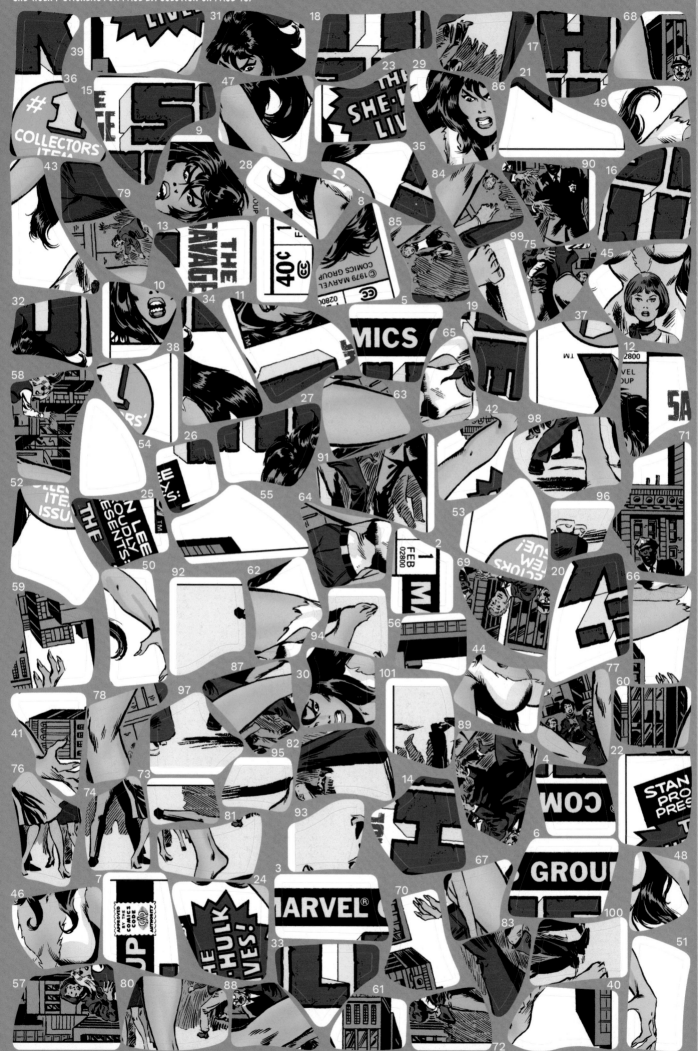

GUARDIANS OF THE GALAXY / STICKERS FOR PAGE 33. SOLUTION ON PAGE 50.